Coffee Break

Let the Truth Sting

Let the Truth Sting

By
The Coffee Lady

Dictionary Content Webster 1848 Dictionary

Copyright 2015 by Letitia Doss
Books Without Borders
Presents
COFFEE BREAK
Let the Truth Sting

Printed in the United States

ISBN 978-0-9967708-0-4

Coffee Break

Dedication

This book is dedicated to the reader, you. Every good and perfect thing comes from the Lord. Therefore, every good idea, plan and thought you had, have, and will have, comes from our Creator. So, just do it until it gets done. Time is on your side as God has redeemed the time. As long as you have life, He has a vessel. In your willingness to yield to His Spirit, He will complete what He began in you. So again, just do it until it gets done.

Please visit *The Coffee Lady's* website, **coffeebr8k.verbal-solutions.com** for more interactive ways to self-discover. You can also order the eBook, *Mini-Coffee Break: House of Love*, which is the prelude to this edition of Coffee Break, directly from the site or at Amazon.com.

Here is a shot of Coffee Break's prelude…

Mini-Coffee Break: House of Love

…Living requires one to go through multiple stages of development. Our maturity involves consistently asking questions pertaining to who we are. Questions are the keys to identity. Can you remember how inquisitive you were as a little girl? Do you recall always asking why? Children are full of questions regarding who they are. What was I like when I was a baby? Where did I come from? How did I get in mommy's stomach? What is this, why does that, who am I, why am I, why, why, why? Nothing satisfies her inquisition more than hearing how special and unique she is. She is always looking to know the unknown. During this stage, the mind is free. It is not connected to any negative experience, therefore it remains open to freely discover. True freedom is discovering the truth of who we are and simply *being* that.

When our curiosity is overtaken, we stop asking questions about who we are. We become comfortable in the environment we create and we choose to remain a habitual survivor. Our desire to continue to self-discover is hindered by the scar of the burn and fear of the stove. No longer do we even want the answers to the questions we now have about the stove. Why did the stove burn me? Why didn't the stove burn everybody else? What is the purpose of the stove? How does the stove really work? The desire to know these answers have been broken by our desire to not be burned again. Therefore, we remain ignorant of truth.

———————————

"Now, it came to pass, as they went, that he entered into a certain village; and a certain woman named Martha received him into her house. And she had a sister called Mary, which also sat at Jesus' feet, and heard his word. But, Martha was cumbered about much serving, and came to and said, Lord, do you not care that my sister has left me to serve alone? Bid her therefore that she help me. And Jesus answered and said to her, Martha, Martha, you are careful and troubled about many, but one is needful and

Mary has chosen good part, which will not be taken away from her."

"*Martha, Martha, you are careful and troubled about many, but one is needful…*" Many of us are just like Martha, careful and troubled about many. We are concerned about many things and many people, more than we are concerned about the One who has ALL the answers to the one who asks. Like Martha, when the Master Builder comes and knocks at our door, we let Him in due to the extent of damage our home has suffered. However, when He explains the process of demolishing the walls covering our pain and fear, the unknown causes us to turn and continue building more walls. We fear bearing in our mind the degree of damage the traumatic experience may reveal. It has been hidden behind so many walls for so long. The sight of it may be too much for us to endure. Although, we are exhausted from the aimless work of building worthless walls, our way is more comfortable than simply letting go. As a result, we make the **choice** to *keep trying* to remain alive instead of *just living.*

"…*Mary has* **chosen** *good part, which will not be taken away from her.*" The Master Builder hid a "good part" in each and every one of us. Good meaning strength that is adequate to support and complete its natural character. Part is a piece separated from the whole. In other words, each of us is fully equipped with adequate strength to support our distinct personality, but our piece needs to be joined back with the whole. Mary recognized, accepted, embraced and confronted her weakness in strength because of the presence of the Master Builder. His presence revealed rest. His presence revealed peace. His presence revealed hope. His presence revealed wholeness. His presence revealed who she had been, was not who she was created to be. This made her want more. So, in the presence of the Master Builder, Mary looked in her mirror and saw her truth. "In me I see He and now I see who I am created to be." Mary not only received Jesus into her home, she chose to sit her tired behind down and listen as He answered her burning question, "WHO AM I?"

We already know who we are and how we function within the walls of our broken home. Yet, who do we become once we welcome the Master Builder in to renovate? Many women are ashamed and disgraced by our truth behind the walls. Shame is a character stain and disgrace is a character flaw. These past character stains and flaws add value to our home once the Master Builder repairs it. The renovation reveals how much the Master Builder truly loves those who are stained and flawed. When we share this good news with others, it gives them hope. Then our remodeled home becomes a house of love for others to meet the Master Builder.

The good news of a free newly remodeled home sounds amazing, doesn't it? Imagine welcoming the Master Builder into our home and taking a seat. Then, He turns to us and lovingly tells us how every part of our life was intended to position us at His feet. Can you feel His arms encasing your body mending all that has been broken? We no longer have to build walls for a home He has already finished constructing. As a matter of fact, every home is complete and fully furnished. Everything from the kitchen appliances, to the bedroom furniture is one of a kind. The renewed walls are now blank canvas left for us to add our own authentic design of colorful artistry. The closets are filled with jewelry and clothing exclusive to each of our individual personality. Finally, to make it all worthwhile, the Master Builder, once and for all, totally cleansed every home with a product that cleanses so well, the home will NEVER get dirty again. The ONLY thing for us to do is accept the home as is! Find out how to get the best use out of all the furniture and appliances. Only wear our own individual apparel and jewelry. ALWAYS open our home to others to see the Master Builder and discover for themselves His love and His purpose of always looking for old homes in desperate need of restoration.

Freedom is the ability to self-discover without the boundaries of others, in order to learn what works personally for each of us. So woman, ask yourself, "Who am I?" Answer, I am He. Now, we must sit down and discover, "Who is He in me?"

Enjoy more of the eBook prelude, *Mini-Coffee Break: House of Love* by ordering it at Amazon.com or at **www.coffeebr8k.verbal-solutions.com**.

Coffee Break

Let the Truth Sting

Inspired by *John 15*...

The Meaning of

Coffee Break: Let the Truth Heal

Coffee – a drink made from the berry of the coffee tree. The berry grows in *clusters*, along the branches, under the *axils* of the leaves (*Cluster* – A number of individuals or things collected or gathered into a close body. *Axils* – In botany, the space or angle formed by a branch with the stem or by a leaf with the stem or branch)

Break – A state of being open, or the act of separating; an opening made by force; an open place. A pause; an interruption; the first appearance of light in the morning; the dawn; as the break of day

Let – to permit; to allow; to suffer; to give leave or power by a positive or negative act, to withhold restraint; not to prevent

Truth – Conformity to fact or reality; the real state of things; exact accordance with that which is, or has been, or shall be; purity from falsehood; honesty, virtue

Sting – a sharp pain; that which gives the principle pain, or constitutes the principle terror.

Coffee Break: Let the Truth Sting – Like the berry of the coffee tree, we grow in clusters (individuals gathered into a close body) under the axils (the space angled and adjoined to the *Stem*). When we pause at the first appearance of *Light* and allow ourselves to be opened for the purpose of separating the positive from the negative, day breaks. It benefits us to give leave or power to the Light and discover the real state of who we are for purification from the lies we have grown to believe. The realization of these facts generates a piercing pain, yet our acceptance of these truths brings on a series of actions that leads us to our destiny.

Let the Truth Sting

This Edition

of

Coffee Break

This edition of Coffee Break consists of the introduction, four breaks, a call to inward & outward action, and a sneak peek of the next edition. The breaks were created to be short reads for the woman who is always on the go yet, needs a break. Each break can be enjoyed while drinking a cup of coffee or one's favorite drink.

Introduction- The Break of Coffee Break – The introduction simply describes the details of the break of Coffee Break and gives a brief description of this edition, *"Let the Truth Sting."*

1st Break- Tall Upside-Down Caramel Macchiato – The 1st Break is named after the first coffee I ever ordered from Starbucks. I began going to Starbucks almost 20 years ago and I have been a faithful customer ever since. This break is tall (small), upside-down with a sweet taste of caramelized sugar. It poses the question, "Why was I created?" and challenges women to seek within not without to discover their answer.

2nd Break- Grande 2 Pump Soy White Mocha – The 2nd Break is named after my absolute favorite Starbucks drink. This break is focused on individual establishment through faith exercises. Faith is one of the strongest emotions. It is the force by which the mind is persuaded. The mind believes and makes evident whatever is consistently repeated, be it the external voices of others or our own internal voice. This break helps build on the strength of the woman's internal voice to re-empower its definitive purpose in her life.

3rd Break- Venti Salted Caramel Vanilla Latte – The 3rd Break is named after a drink I once tried but, did not particularly care for, at least not *at first*. This break is a large dose of salty sweetness. The initial taste is first bitter, but then it transitioned into this reassuring delightfulness leaving the pallet wanting more. This salted yet, sweet break gives the woman a glimpse of her mirrored truth.

Final Break- Straight Double Espresso – The Final Break is a straight-up extra-strong dose of forward movement. I order this drink when I don't *feel* like doing what I know I am purposed to do. Learning is great, but has no value unless it is applied properly. In this break knowledge is challenged by belief. We may know what it takes to acquire a thing, but no woman is ready to acquire that thing until she believes God created her to subdue it. This Final Break is to support, protect, and respire the truth of that mirrored woman.

"Me Time" & "Me First" – These sections are to call women to action. It is my hope that after women read these breaks they are inspired to ask and seek to find their true purpose in life. 'Me Time' is a call to personal action for women to see themselves as God sees them and to speak what God has spoken *of* them. 'Me First' is a call to outward action. It gives a lesson, teaching women to Love self first, in order to truly be able to give Love away to others. Loving 'me first' doesn't mean women learn to love only 'me…' Loving 'me first' deepens a woman's love for everyone else and cultivates her desire to passionately give to others what she has given to herself.

The Next Sip - Black Coffee No Sugar No Cream – The Next Sip is just that, a little taste of the second edition of Coffee Break. Forest Gump said it best, "Love is what Love does." Therefore, we need to really know what Love is so that we are able to truly do what Love does.

Coffee Break

TABLE OF CONTENTS

Let the Truth Sting

The Break of Coffee Break

Coffee Break was inspired by every woman who has ever taken a break with me. It started with going to Starbucks to get to know the women in my life. Over time, two of my sister-friends made it into a joke and started calling me *The Coffee Lady*. They would tell people if you ever go to Starbucks with *The Coffee Lady*, expect to cry. Coffee Breaks eventually turned into any time spent getting to know another apart from the norm. Taking a Coffee Break doesn't necessarily mean a break while drinking coffee. It's taking a break from the everyday hustle and bustle of life. Whether the break is over a drink, a meal, a conference, an overnight hotel getaway, a spa, a vacation, a movie, shopping or chilling at the park – we all deserve and need a Coffee Break. What was discovered during these coffee breaks was not only do we need a break from life and everyday routines, but we also need something to break within. An internal break is necessary in order to gain a deeper revelation and better understanding of who we are, and what we are created to do.

"*He (she) shall be like a tree planted by the rivers of water that brings forth its fruit in its season, whose leaf also shall not wither; and whatever he (she) does shall prosper*." Psalms 1:3

Before a seed can be planted, the ground has to be tilled. Breaking ground is considered breaking the mold of habit to do something different. Once the ground is broken and moistened by water (tears), the seed can be planted. When seeds are placed in moistened ground another break takes place, sprouting of roots. This is the break within or the transformation for taking root. The deeper the roots grow, the stronger the tree will become. Before tree sprouts breakthrough the ground for the great reveal, their roots grow down prior to growing up. Rain (tears) is an essential element needed to continue softening and moistening the ground to bring forth change and newness of life. After the sprout has been developed in darkness, it emerges to be exposed by the Light. The rays of the Sun shine bright to regulate the temperature and mature the budding tree so it may open up and reveal its unique beauty. As the seasons change, the various weather conditions anchor the roots and develop the true nature of the tree. The tree's unique and invaluable splendor is identified by the substance of its produce, fruit. Finally, the tree matures and experiences ongoing seasons of harvest and others are able to enjoy the true radiance and spirit of its fruit, permanent prosperity.

This edition of *Coffee Break: Let the Truth Sting* will be a break of truth. Our own individual truth makes us free and in our freedom we have the option to choose life or death. It is my hope and prayer that the revelation of your truth will free you from the lies put on you by life experiences, yourself, and others. Enjoy this *Coffee Break* and get to know you first. *Let the Truth Sting* your wounds as God reveals who you truly are in Him. Then, take Coffee Breaks with other women and get to know the true essence of who they really are as well.

Coffee Break

Let the Truth Sting

Tall Upside Down Caramel Macchiato

"Wisdom is the principal thing; therefore get wisdom: and with all thy getting get understanding." Proverb 4:7 KJV

Living a life of Jesus Christ is a progressive process. Process is defined as a series of actions and motions or changes in growth causing forward movement. As we process, we gradually move forward on a progressive course toward a place where we are destined to be. Simply stated, progressive movement is when we advance forward proceeding with improvement. Mathematics would be considered a progressive process subject. In preschool, a child must first learn to recognize numbers before they can count. They then need to understand the value of numbers before they learn to add them. Once they know how to add, they are ready to move forward and learn subtraction, multiplication, division and so on. In mathematics, the key to a progressive process depends on understanding the purpose of numbers. The same is true in our Christian walk. We need an understanding of the true nature of God, His love for us and our purpose for being created.

Every created being is purposed by God. Operating in our unique greatness is contingent upon us understanding who the Creator is, why He created us, and most importantly, how to totally surrender our lives to His perfect will. There is a point in life when everyone asks the inevitable question, "Why was I created?" For the Christ follower, this is a fully loaded question that requires direct instructions or it will be aimed and fired in the long direction. Yes, long direction not wrong direction. A true follower of Christ will indeed fulfill their God given purpose and what may appear to be the wrong direction is actually the long direction. For example, the Israelites were in the wilderness for 40 years instead of the 11 days it should have taken them to make it to the Promised Land. The journey was long, but in the end they made it. Jesus was full of wisdom and teaching at 12 years old, yet it wasn't until He was 30 when He began His public ministry. The journey was long, but He fulfilled it. Sometimes what we interpret as the wrong way is really just the long way. This long way to godly wisdom and understanding can sometimes be described as the most uncomfortable level of discomfort.

One day I re-read one of my old journals and the Lord revealed the revelation of my progressive process. The journal was laden with tests, trials and extremely poor decision making. However, as I read the final entry of the journal I heard a still small voice say, "*You're still standing.*" It was at that moment the clarity of Proverbs 4:7 was made evident in my life. *Wisdom is the principal thing; therefore get wisdom: and with all thy getting get understanding.* The Webster 1828 dictionary defines wisdom as the right use or exercise of knowledge. The *right use of knowledge* is vital, therefore get *the right use of knowledge*, and with all the getting of *exercised knowledge*, find out the real state of things presented, *understanding*. We can only rightly use what we know by understanding

35

the real state of what is presented before us. It is through understanding the value of a number (the real state) that teaches a child how to rightly use the number, not just knowing what the number is. In essence, we need to know and understand our real value. We may not always understand the real state of what God is allowing to be presented in our lives. Therefore, we should seek Him for the right use of knowledge and trust that He will give understanding as we continue to exercise His knowledge. We will not always rightly use God's knowledge. Truth be told, there will be times when we blatantly ignore Him and act out of self. Nevertheless, continuously seeking God, in spite of our actions, will cause us to gradually advance forward with intentional improvement guiding us to our destined place. But, we must first ask the inevitable question, "Why was I created?"

The Creator is the only one who can and will answer this question. He's the only One who knows our true purpose and the only One who has the key to unlocking our understanding. Jesus is not a respecter of persons. What He has done for one, He will freely do for all who sincerely ask. He will reveal your truth and purpose just as He has revealed mine. As you read the pages of this process, pray and ask God to bless you with His wisdom and understanding for your God given purpose.

Coffee Break

Let the Truth Sting

Grande 2 Pump Soy White Mocha

"…I know we will…"

Wow, what confidence and trust! This is a quote I used to declare that my husband and I will work through any and every situation to become a godly example for other marriages. I spoke these words with sheer confidence December 2001. What's clear today, which wasn't then, is in order to be an example one must be made a pattern for others to learn by. It takes creativity, keen detail, time, and patience to craft a pattern. God, being all that and more, revealed to me years ago that our marriage would be a pattern of "*two becoming one*" in Christ. Well, being shaped into a pattern by God requires cutting, forming and being molded to look like Christ, to behave like Christ, so others can see Christ through you. At this point, I truly believe, nothing is impossible for God. Through my marriage He has shown me endless possibilities and I am utterly amazed. My husband and I have been through many trials, we have overcome much tribulation, with even more to come. But, through it all, God has shown Himself faithful. I remember my late pastor and father, Reginald A. Caldwell, Senior saying "You're either on your way in, just got out or walking through the valley." Unbeknown back in December 2001, a valley was approaching. It's amazing how easy it is to have unwavering faith in God when we are "*happy*" or when things are going well in our lives. Yet, how do we learn to lean and totally depend on Christ as we are going through the storm? Faith exercises. God has given each of us a measure of faith (Romans 12:3) and the measure that we receive needs regular exercise in order to grow stronger. *Now faith is the substance of things hoped for, the evidence of things not seen* (Hebrews 11:1). Faith precedes hope. Faith inspires hope. We should apply faith to every circumstance. Faith is best exercised as we walk through our valley experiences. In the valley, we cannot see the evidence of the mountain top. However, the valley is where we learn how to carefully apply God's promises to our situation.

The purpose of exercise is to increase energy to continue onward. Exercising faith helps to develop other key components, which we need to apply as we continue to move toward God. Only God can complete what He began in us and He will by faith. When faith is exercised regularly, it produces Christian energy. Remember how energetic you were after first becoming a Christian? Upon salvation, we are so moved by it and driven that we think we are fully equipped to preach the Gospel and save the whole world. We don't realize the need to continuously exercise our faith to increase energy. Christian energy is the power exerted by the Spirit of Jesus. We have the power to seek God first, the power to intercede, the power to speak life one to another, the power to stand strong, the power to endure and the power to be victorious in all things. God's power is endless and properly exercising our Christian energy will generate godly knowledge.

Misguided energy will lose its force without knowledge, causing complacency. Knowing how to apply God's Word and applying it by belief, stirs up the energy to keep moving forward. Forward progress stimulates our spiritual senses to give us understanding of the Scriptures. Proverbs 1:7 tells us that fearing the Lord is the beginning of knowledge. I remember first learning about the fear of the Lord and I thought God wanted us to be scared of Him so we wouldn't sin. Initially, everyone has a negative association of fearing God because of our lack of understanding. Yet, the fear of the Lord is an extremely sacred regard for God that stems from a sincere love of His divine character. It's not fear in the sense of being afraid, it's respect and affection for Him loving us in spite of our condition and choices. When we know this, we are effectively exercising God's knowledge and these exercises eventually produce self-control.

As our spiritual intellect is sharpened by the knowledge of God, we learn how to restrain ourselves from indulging in ungodly behavior through submitting. *Submit yourselves therefore to God. Resist the devil, and he will flee from you* (James 4:7). God stands against the devil (all evil), interrupting its progress in our lives, as we submit to Him. Giving our minds over to the Spirit frees us from the bondage of sin, causing us to acknowledge our righteousness. The more we believe of God, the more we desire to please Him. The more we desire to please God, the more we surrender our self-controlled will to God's will. When we exercise self-control, it will produce the most genuine form of patience and endurance.

Our Heavenly Father loves to show Himself powerful and faithful in every situation. God is looking for us to have a calm temper through the suffering of afflictions and through the pangs of life. This reveals His sovereignty and shows we truly believe He has already done what He said He would do. Jesus exhibited this characteristic at, what I believe to be, the most excruciating time of His earthly walk, Calvary. His mind agreed with His heart, He understood the greater purpose, and He saw victory. There is no need for us to react to the storm. With patience and endurance we begin to allow the Holy Spirit to respond from our hearts, which aligns our minds to God's will. In this, Jesus gives peace that surpasses understanding, so that we may fully exercise patience and endurance, which produces purity.

God's purification frees us from guilt and the pollution of sin. Guilt causes us to think that suffering affliction is a penalty that requires compensation. The truth is we can never, not ever, repay God for the ultimate sacrifice of His only begotten Son, Jesus. That sacrifice freed us from guilt, sin and our misguided views of righteousness. Doing the "right thing" doesn't make us right in the sight of God. The free gift of righteousness (grace) is godly purity at its best and there is only One Way to obtain it, through Christ. *Jesus saith unto him, I am the way, the truth, and the life; no man cometh unto the Father, but by me* (John 14:6). Sin completely separates the created from the Creator, but God! The Lord is so merciful, so full of compassion, so forgiving, has and will continue to suffer so long with each one of us, because He loves us so. Love covers an indefinite amount of sin and God's love is not limited by our condition. With our Father's love, Jesus' selfless sacrifice, and the power of the Holy Spirit, we are made whole and are cleansed from all unrighteousness, purified. Purity is exercised in believing that we are being led by the Holy Spirit and by His leading we freely extend brotherly affection.

Our relation to God the Father is through the spirit of adoption led by our brother, Jesus. Jesus modeled brotherly affection by laying down His life. *Hereby perceive we the love of God, because He laid down His life for us; and we ought to lay down our lives for the brethren* (1 John 3:16). This is humility at the height of humility. There is truly no greater love than this. Christ humbled Himself, gave up all power and authority in heaven, to save a world destined for eternal death. He did not come to save the holier than thou, traditional, ritualistic, 8-day-a-week-church-going, always got it together, non-sinning believer. Neither did He come to condemn the drug addicted, sexually active, non-married, gender confused, lying, thieving, once a year church going believer or non-believer. Jesus came to seek and save those who are lost (Luke 19:10) and by His Spirit, we are to do the same thing. The lost are those who can't find their way to the Truth, those who are unloved, confused, mislead, forgotten and despised. Once we come into the knowledge of Love's Truth, we are willing to lovingly lay down our lives for one another, exercising brotherly affection, leading us to generously give Christian love.

Christlike love is to earnestly love another without conditions. Everyone wants to be loved and no matter what we do right, wrong or indifferent, we still desire to be handled with gentle kind affection. Jesus commanded us to love one another the exact same way He has loved us (John 13:34-35). Let's examine that. How long has Jesus suffered with our iniquities? How gentle and kind is He toward us when we keep messing up in the same area? How much does He rejoice when we overcome what others would consider a tiny victory? How many times has He just thrown in the towel? NEVER! (1 Corinthians 13:4-8) We can go on and on about Love's unconditional faithfulness. This is the exact same way we are to love one another. When the heart loves it doesn't give up, no matter what. Loving another means being gentle and kind while they are experiencing the growing pains of life. During their growing pains, love shows up and cares for them, gives to them and trusts God through the process. Remember, Love doesn't acknowledge the sins of others; it covers the sins and only identifies the good in them. Therefore, we are to see and respond to the good in others. This is especially true and has the greatest effect when the good in them is not clearly visible. Committed love sees the good through the murky water and focuses only on that. We should not react to the false state of those who are simply looking to be loved, but we should choose to see the good (God's Truth) in them. God's Word remains true despite sin. God saw all He created and it was very good (Genesis 1:31). Therefore, we have the ability, if we choose to do the same, to see all He has created as being good and very good.

Every situation comes to exercise our faith, virtue, knowledge, self-control, patience, purity, brotherly affection and Christian love for the purpose of prospering us, keeping us from being idle and unfruitful (1 Peter 1:5-8). These characteristics are who Jesus is and should become a major part of who we are as Christ followers. Since the dawn of our marriage, these types of faith exercises have been the pattern God uses to fashion me and my husband. And, He will continue to build our marital muscles by faith, molding us to a model of "*two becoming one*" in Christ. I declare, through Christ Jesus, we will *never* fail.

Coffee Break

Venti Salted Caramel Vanilla Latte

"Woe unto them that are wise in their own eyes, and prudent in their own sight!" Isaiah 5:21 KJV

I was once a *"wise in their own eyes"* kind of person. There was a time where my wisdom was based on very limited and untrained knowledge. With little to no exercise in the area of faith and Christian energy, I used to judge the false state of others, especially my husband. It was hard to see the good *in* him, as I was constantly looking for what I wasn't getting *from* him. I considered myself to be a woman who loved the Lord and desired to be pleasing in His sight. So I set my sight solely on learning and doing what I learned about Him. There was much hearing of the Word, but not enough understanding and believing *of* what was heard and the energy was dutiful, but lacked an incredibly necessary quality, *grace*. Self examination is a requirement to truly possess grace. Something I did but, only in part. As time goes on, we will eventually see the painfully obvious need to thoroughly self examine, a valuable trait to have on our Christian journey (1 Corinthians 11:28).

One of the challenges to examining self is having the keen ability to judge ourselves not based on how we appear to others, but according to the true state of our own heart. What is the true condition of our heart? We can't see the real state of anyone's heart except our own and our true heart is what actually matters to God. An accurate evaluation of freedom is the only way to assess the true state of who we are. Therefore, we have to ask ourselves, do we really desire to be made free? And, are we willing to accept the whole truth and nothing but the truth, so help us God? If the answer is yes let the self examination begin. *Heavenly Father, unveil our individual truth in Jesus name...Amen.*

"Examine me, O LORD, and prove me; try my reins and my heart." Psalms 26:2

Deep down each of us have an earnest desire to know, understand, believe and trust our own truth. Our spirits require it, but we need God to inspect us carefully so we may know and understand the real condition of who we are. The truth *makes* us free. Truth frees us from lies, deceit, pretense and selfish-ambition. The truth cuts deep into our flesh and empowers our spirit. If we continue to pursue the Word God imprinted on our individual heart, He will continue to expose our truth. God's plan for each of our lives is hidden in our heart. Only He knows the plans and those plans are for good not evil (Jeremiah 29:11). Many of us cringe when we hear the word "expose." We dislike being vulnerable, but our vulnerability summons the presence of God. Take a moment and really think about that. When we (the children of God) are completely opened and exposed (weakened in the flesh), the true state of who we are calls forth the presence of the Holy Spirit to move on our behalf. We don't have to open our mouths and say one word. The mere state of who we are, by authority of our dependency, notifies God causing Him to appear at that specified place. Yes, you read that correctly: *authority of our dependency*. Our authority is contingent upon our dependency on God and we are completely dependent upon Him when we surrender and totally believe what He says about us. Children of God have legal power and possession over the whole earth and everything in it. Sounds good doesn't it? Well, why do many of us seldom experience the fullness of said power? It's because most of us only believe *in* and not *of*. I'll explain the uniqueness of the two later. The bottom line here is, our Heavenly Father can only restore to health what we allow Him to expose. He is a gentleman. God will never force His way in to change what we are not willing to surrender. Force entry goes against our free will, so we must self-examine and then, give it over to Him. As we go further into the intimate portraits of our life, take the time to examine self and trust that God's love is capable of totally sealing what He reveals. I say *we* as I take this *Coffee Break* because I am still examining myself and discovering more of my truths along the way.

Everyone's truth is different, but how we examine ourselves is very similar. The Lord would never withhold any good thing from us. He wants us to inquire in His temple. Where is His temple? We are His temple (1 Corinthians 3:16). Self-examining is simply inquiring within. The Lord desires for us to inquire within, not without. Guard your heart (Proverbs 4:23). That means protect it from any outer thing that will object to what is already present inside the heart. The knowledge of who God is lives within each of us. *He desires to open the eyes of our heart that we may be enlightened to know the hope of His calling, the riches of the glory of His inheritance and the surpassing greatness of His power toward us who believe* (Ephesians 1:17-19). He's delighted when we dwell in His secret place, seeking Him for truth and allowing His truth to prune us and make us free. The Lord's truth is sovereign and nothing can stand against it. When the mind begins to stray from it, His love will gently guide us back to it. As we seek God, He increases our ability to carefully inspect our being with a panoramic view of the true state of how He has strategically formed our heart. Sometimes in order to get a panoramic view of our true state, we need to step back from what we have been used to doing to see the healing truth. The truth does not hurt! That's a lie planted for us to believe. It may be uncomfortable, but it doesn't hurt. The lies we believe are inflicted wounds that cause pain as we face and embrace our truth. So in all actuality, lies hurt, truth heals.

I remember getting scrapes and cuts from playing outside as a little girl. My late paternal grandmother, Elizabeth, would use this antiseptic called Mecuricome. I hated it! No matter how gentle she was in applying it to the cut, it burned like nothing I had ever felt. She was so patient in comforting me, blowing the wound to try and make it feel better, but nothing helped the sting. I often wondered why she, this woman who loved me so, would use such a painful medicine on an open cut, which I thought to be red hot dye. Then, one day the strangest thing happened. I was playing in her medicine cabinet and I decided to put some red hot dye on my hand where there was no cut or scrape. I was pleasantly surprised to discover that the red hot dye did not burn or sting at all. When the red hot dye was applied to the true state of the body, it didn't sting. It only hurt when applied to a wounded area. When our flesh is open and exposed the application of God's Word stings and causes us to want to run the other way. Although God patiently and gently applies His Word to our wounds, we are still affected by the sting of our truth. However, as we steadily endure the pain, we persevere, which builds our true character. The true character of our hearts is revealed when we allow God to heal our wounded body for the purpose of us living in purpose. It would be wise of us to face our truth quickly before the wound grows outer layers of dry rough scabs. Depending on how deep the wound, the scabs may need to be reopened. The red hot dye doesn't sting when applied to a deep wound covered by a scab. However, it will be very painful when applied to a reopened wound.

When my husband and I met, I was an already deeply wounded woman. Yet, my wounds were protected by scabs. Scabs form to prevent infection and contamination. I believe God allowed this process to avoid further damage to the wound until it was time to reopen it for total healing. For years the very essence of who I thought I was, was based on a misconception of my true identity. Like most Christians, I was wounded by past abuse and misjudged by the enemy as being weak and feeble. Abuse be it physical, mental, emotional, spiritual or sexual has a daunting effect on those who have been polluted by it. Many people live their whole lifetime never receiving the total healing needed to reach their full potential because of abuse. The sexual abuse I endured was intended to break me beyond repair and for a long time it did well in the perception of brokenness. But, I thank God He let my wounds scab to prevent me from becoming an infected contaminated woman. Unfortunately, a deeply scabbed cut has to be reopened to mend, which may be more painful than the initial injury. It is God's desire that we embrace this process as He reopens the wound and allow Him to apply the Mecuricome (His Word). In doing this, we are able to be healed and begin to produce good fruit. When we completely see our heart with ALL its true characteristics (wounds and all), God is then able to shape and mold it into the intended image of Christ. I believe those who are the most judgmental are just people who have wounds that never properly healed and are covered with scabs.

All of my learning about God and doing what I learned eventually led me to resentment, because it was not grounded in the true state of my purposeful identity. My doing was grounded in obligation, causing me to measure what I was doing with what others were not doing. Sadly, my husband was typically the target. I frequently judged what I didn't understand for lack of not getting what I thought I needed from him. My judgment was comparison based. I compared what I did to what he didn't do. In my mind most times I thought I did the "right thing." It took me years to learn that God was illuminating my true identity through him and vice versa ("*two becoming one*"). As we grew closer, his reflection uncovered my wounds and my reflection uncovered his. The more I looked at him, the more God revealed my truth. When two become one, they must enter into a unified state by changing their previous state and assume the new character of the one state.

Take Detroit, Las Vegas and Seattle for example. These three cities have distinct weather conditions that vary tremendously during the winter. Living in Detroit one must learn to adjust to its extreme winter weather. Detroiters experience severely long winters with lots of snow, clouds and brutally cold temperatures that sink well below 0 degrees. Las Vegas is totally opposite as their winters are short, mild and sunny. There is some mountain snow, but snow is rare in Las Vegas with moderately warm temperatures rarely reaching, less known dropping below,

20 degrees. Being from either of these cities, one's winter behavior would have to drastically change to live through the rainy winters in Seattle. Seattle winters are cool, cloudy and wet. There is some snowfall, but rain rules everything around Seattle. It is the rainiest city in the U. S. There is no need to compare Detroit's snow boots and skull caps to Las Vegas' sandals and sunglasses. In Seattle the state of *"two becoming one"* requires umbrellas and rain coats. This applies to becoming one with *anyone* who is in Christ. As we are coming together we have to leave behind what worked for us in our previous state and look to Jesus for what works in our new present state. Seeing the false state of another is God's way of focusing our attention on Jesus, to reveal the true state of who He created us to be as individuals, therefore, showing us how to sincerely love others as Christ loves us.

Straight Double Espresso

Progressive Process – Onward Mobility

In order to shift further, one must believe what is said to be positioned ahead. There are things God says are ahead of us as individuals and as a collective Body and we must believe to see those things naturally manifest. With a mind toward God let us ask ourselves the question, what do we believe? Now, this may or may not seem to be an easy question with an easy answer. However, take a little time and evaluate what is in the heart, then check to see if the mind is in total agreement with it. As the question fills the mind, look at the areas of your life where you might feel hindered or stuck. We may possibly be held-up in places where we know God has promised us things due to unbelief or misguided belief. Knowing the promises of God are of no effect if we don't believe the promises God has specifically made toward us. We can search the Scriptures and learn all the promises of the Heavenly Father, all the miracles of Jesus, and all the authority and power of the Holy Spirit, but if we don't know to believe what we know it means for us as individuals, our knowledge of all these truths are meaningless.

One of my favorite things to say when someone is going through… "When things get rough always remember a Word you know to be true and apply it in spite of how you feel and what you see." Those of us who love to learn have a true love for knowledge. We want to know and understand in order to apply what we have learned to our everyday lives, which in all actuality is wisdom. Taken in its original context, wisdom is good as we understand how to submit to what we know. For me, this statement derived from the love *of* knowledge and the desire to submit to what's right no matter what. Knowing God's truth and how to apply His Word to my life has been the basis of my Christian walk. This may sound good, but, it's not what we know that carries us to our destiny; it's what we *know* to believe. If we know too much, we may begin to believe too much of the wrong thing. Right now, I'm realizing how uninformed my favorite statement is when considering what belief means. This principle has been applied to my life for the past fourteen years and lately I've been questioning its accuracy leading me to ask God why. His reply was simple, "You know more about Me than you believe *of* Me." It was interesting to me how God used "believe *of*" Him instead of "believe *in*" Him so I looked up the words *of* and *in* and was truly enlightened.

To be *in* something is to be *present* or *surrounded by* it, such as, being *in* the city of Detroit. Being *in* the city of Detroit places limits on how far one can go in order to remain *in* that city. Once the city line is crossed, one enters another city and is then *out* of the city of Detroit. However, to be *of* something is to be *proceeding from* or *out of* it, such as, being *of* the city of Detroit. The city by which we are born is where we are *of* and no matter how many city lines we cross we will always be *of* or from that city. There is no way to not be *of* that city despite where we go. That is the city by which we were produced. I was born and raised *of* the city of Detroit. That's where I am from and regardless to where I travel or even live, I will always be *of* (from) the city of Detroit. Accordingly, believing *of* God means what we believe *proceeds from* and *out of* Him. In spite of how much we learn about God, it will not cause us to crossover or move out of what we "believe *of*" Him, as our belief advances from Him. God becomes the source of what we believe and in the process He gives knowledge, understanding, and wisdom according to the internal sketches of our individual heart. His knowledge, understanding, and wisdom of who He created us to be should flow from the inner most parts *of* our previously formed heart, not *in* what we know we've learned to behave *in*.

For example, the Bible provides great principles for how to be a godly wife. A woman can seek to learn and apply all of these wonderful truths successfully to her marriage based off her knowledge in God's Word. But, what God specifically sketched on her heart is how she is to submit to her own husband, as to the Lord (Ephesians 5:22). She and her husband are unique and by God's design He created the one for the other. In order for her to submit to her own husband, as to the Lord, her mind must fully align with her own purposely created heart, so that her submission will proceed from belief *of* God to her husband and not derive from knowledge *in* God. There are specific promises made to specific people throughout the Bible. Those who received God's promises for them believed of Him and became one with His purpose for their lives. When we believe of Him and search the internal sketches of our own heart, the Spirit unveils the promises God has spoken distinctively for us. The interior sketches of our heart (God's Truth concerning our being), have to align with our mind, which in turn gives us the mind of Christ. Once the mind completely agrees with the heart, it is then wholly unified of God. The key to reaching our full potential and having unlimited access to our fearfully and wonderfully made inward parts is to "believe *of* Him." My belief had been stagnate as it was misguided being *in* (surrounded by) knowledge about God and not *of* (proceeding from) God. Just like being in the city of Detroit places limits on how far one can go to remain in the city, believing in God, solely based on knowledge, limits how far we are able to advance in the Kingdom of God (righteousness, peace, joy in the Holy Spirit).

Always knowing what to do and how to do may begin to spark determination and discipline, resulting in being one who knows how to get the job done. Yet, determination and discipline are attributes of a strong mind and will. Having a strong self-will places limits on God's will. We become so determined to do things the way we see it that it prevents the Spirit from doing things the way God purposed it. Eventually, something happens along the way and we begin to realize how we have been experiencing restricted advancement. However, we still find ourselves saying things like "I'm pressing forward" or "I'm believing God for this or that," so we continue in the long direction. But, what happens along the way when we are stalled in our beliefs of what we learned is to come? What happens when we get to the place where we meet back up with unbelief, the place in our walk when we say "if You" to our Lord? *But if You can do anything…"* (Mark 9:22). Lord, "if You" can do anything with my habits, my marriage, my love, my finances, my children, my desires, my ministry, my health, my life have compassion and assist me. Lord, "if You" love me or "if You" hear me or "if You" are real… At this very instant I am at an "if You" moment in my life. This has shocked me to say the least, as I had considered myself to be someone who was strong in faith. However, I have been showing signs of weakened faith for some time now and didn't know it. "If You" has been in my mind toward the one person I claim to love the most, my husband. Let me be clear on what I wholeheartedly believe. I believe once we *wholeheartedly* accept Jesus Christ as our Lord and Savior, He dwells within us and immediately we are made one with Him. We are, at that moment, who He says and we have what He possesses totally and completely in heart. Yet, our minds take more convincing to become one mind with Christ. This being said, the Holy Spirit dwells in my husband and He in him do I love the most in this world. So how did I arrive at this place of weakened faith inadvertently holding "if You" in my mind?

"If You…"

It's interesting how much these words are thrown at the One who is able to do exceeding abundantly above ALL we ask or imagine, according to the power that works *in us* (Ephesians 3:20). "If" implies whether or not. It is a sign of something being conditional and provisional. To say "if You" insinuates there is a possibility of can't. We may *know* God to be limitless, eternal and we may *know* there is nothing He can't do. We may *know* His love is unconditional and He never changes. We may *know* we are created in His image and it is Him who wills and works through us for His good pleasure. We may *know* all of these things and yet still stagger at His promises through unbelief. Our minds need to be *fully persuaded* that God is able to perform His promises for our lives.

"He staggered not at the promise of God through unbelief; but was strong in faith, giving glory to God. And being fully persuaded that, what He had promised, He was able also to perform. And therefore it was imputed to him for righteousness. Now it was not written for his sake alone, that it was imputed to him; but for us also, to whom it shall be imputed, if we believe on Him that raised up Jesus our

Lord from the dead; Who was delivered for our offenses and raised again for our justification." (Romans 4:20-25)

Abraham *knew* that both he and Sarah were past childbearing age, and He *knew* no one who had borne children during their stage of life, yet he was *fully persuaded.* His belief in what God had or had not done before was not predicated on all the promises he *knew* of God, but He aligned his mind to match the promise God made specifically to him. God promised Abraham a child and Abraham simply agreed with God, in spite of what he did or did not know.

"And Jesus said to him, "If you can! All things are possible for one who believes." Immediately the father of the child cried out and said, 'I believe; help my unbelief.'" Mark 9:23-24

"...I believe; help my unbelief..."

Knowledge challenges belief. Belief challenges knowledge. Knowledge opposes belief. Belief opposes knowledge. Knowledge defies belief. Belief defies knowledge. Knowing is not half the battle, *it is the battle*. We have to unlearn what we know in order to truly believe who we are in Jesus. I know the abuse of my childhood damaged my esteem well into my thirties. I know the promiscuity in my teens caused a multitude of unhealthy soul ties that led me to adultery. I know my adulteress actions broke trust in my marriage, which induced my husband's infidelity. Most importantly, I know the series of these events led me to question my belief. Knowledge is power and that power can cause our minds to believe we are the product of our environment. The knowledge of our situation defies the belief of who God created us to be. The Creator has a perfect knowledge of all His works. He knows exactly who we are, and He is waiting for us to seek Him to believe His truth concerning us. We, on the other hand, have limited knowledge based on personal experiences. The exposure of our truth provides a break in our limited knowledge. Limited knowledge needs to be broken for God's perfect knowledge to inspire our belief. The knowledge of God's truth of who I am challenged my belief, in order to renew my mind, so I could be fully persuaded. The mind has to agree with what God sketched in our hearts. Properly defined, belief is the act of admitting and agreeing with the truth of a plan by which the mind is ABSOLUTELY convinced of that truth. Belief is meant to persuade the mind of the truth (forward advancement), which is founded on the internal imprints of our heart and not based on what we know personally. Our mind requires evidence in order to fully embrace the truth of our heart. We simply need to ask, what is God's perfect plan for me? Then, we must choose to allow our minds to recognize and correspond to God's plan. Once the mind identifies with what God positioned in the heart, we are able to move forward as He intended without limits.

Today, as I close this Coffee Break, I can sincerely say that I am now *fully persuaded* and I fully believe who I am: a fearfully and wonderfully made woman of God. However, I also understand that I will consistently face my truth as I continue to grow in Christ. My prayer for you is that you Let the Truth Sting to break any personal knowledge and allow God's perfect knowledge to renew your mind, rightly aligning it to your heart, so you may believe you are who God says you are.

Coffee Break

Let the Truth Sting

"Me Time"

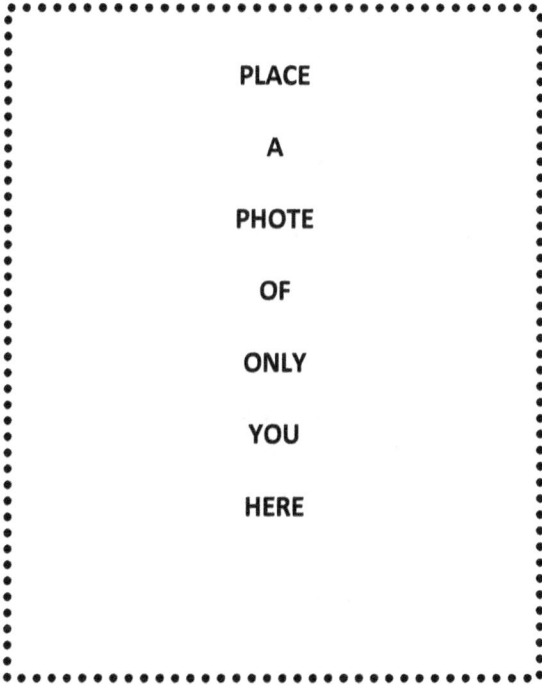

PLACE

A

PHOTE

OF

ONLY

YOU

HERE

THEN,

Take a "Me Time" break and encourage that amazing
woman in the mirror…

Recite this poem to yourself in a mirror until you believe it!

Beautiful Me

I AM beautiful.
I AM amazing.
I AM powerful.
I AM majestic.
I AM creative.
I AM strong.
I AM intelligent.
I AM interesting.
I AM unique.
I AM priceless.
I AM exceptional.
I AM extraordinary.
I AM important.
I AM precious.
I AM valuable.
I AM royalty
I AM loved.
I AM FREE!

I have survived, NOW it is time FOR ME to live.

I AM beautifully, wonderfully and exceptionally made in the image of the King of kings. Once I accepted the Savior of all humankind, Jesus Christ, I was immediately received into the best family ever, as a child of the Most High. I AM His child and He loves me more than words can ever describe. There is nothing I can ever do, no place I can ever go, and nothing I can ever say, that will stop Him from loving me. His thoughts are forever toward me and it brings Him the greatest joy when I ask Him about me. Anything that opposes what He says about me is simply not true.

Let the Truth Sting

"Me First"

Upon our entry into this world we are first identified by gender. It's a girl! Joy fills the air. However, the joy of having a girl does not equate to that girl being joyful. As a matter of fact, if asked, a woman full of joy may tell you that her road to joy was not as pleasant as she'd hoped. Probably since the beginning of time girls have been raised to serve others. One of the first toys a young girl receives is a doll. Immediately, she is emerged into a world of caring for others. From there, it's off to her toy kitchen with her toy grocery cart where she shops, cooks, and irons, within minutes, for her make believe family in a boa and plastic toy heeled shoes. Her imagination is then filled with ideas of being wedded to prince charming by the classic princess stories she has grown accustomed to. She settles into her teens with worries of self-imagery. Her true potential is limited by the ideas of trendy fashion, flawless makeup, primped hair styles, and a body of an airbrushed magazine model. She then ventures out into the real world trying to discover the true essence of who she is only to be redirected back to caring for others first. As the years roll by, questions of marriage and children are often asked by family and friends during family gatherings and class reunions. She dare not say, these things are not a priority, nor that she wants to discover herself before settling into others' expectations of what she's capable of giving them. She dare not say to those whom she loves, honors, and respects, *me first*. That's absurd! Or is it?

She can hear their thoughts saying, "Well, that's selfish. She's only thinking of herself. Who does she think she is? Doesn't she know the importance of family? Living life is more about helping others than about helping self." She can already feel their eyes piercing at her in disbelief with their noses flared with disapproval. Yet, in the secret compartments of her heart she holds tightly to her truth *me first*. For years she has watched women pour all of what they had out to others leaving nothing for themselves. It hurts her to see women who were often heavy laden with guilt for ever attempting to do something solely for them, especially after they had given so much to those they loved. Her own mother was married with children by the time she was twenty-one and sacrificed all of her hopes and dreams for her family. Every now and then she sees a spark of hope gleaming in her mother's eyes, but it vanishes quickly as soon as her mother realizes someone else wants her help. During one of those moments, she made up her mind that she would start with *me first*. She didn't want to put her hopes and dreams on the low end of her priorities, as she believed that what she wanted was just as much of a priority as anyone else. So, she started to fill her own tank with what she believed to be the most vital necessity in life, Love.

What she found was Love came to her rescue and was more fulfilling than any prince charming could ever be. Love taught her how to be first kind, warm, and gentle toward the one whose reflection existed in the mirror. Then, once she fully understood and accepted the reflection, she would be able to extend those same attributes to others, particularly those who appeared to be most difficult. She realized that the most difficult people are the way they are because they have yet to discover the true concept of Love. This realization stirred within her a level of patience, which can only be obtained with an ample supply of condition-less Love. She learned first not to judge her own conditions, neither the conditions of others as Love taught her that every cause has an effect. The more skilled she became with loving her own image, the more Love grew. The more Love grew within her, the more she realized that she wanted to give Love away to others. She fell deeper and deeper into Love as she matured into the true character of her being. Self-acceptance was embraced and heightened, while Love enveloped and sealed every part of her existence, all the way down to her shadow. At last, she has been known by Love, and finally she loves Love. Now, she can fully accept the mirrored reflection of the girl transformed into a woman. The lenses of Love cleared her vision, and as she considers her journey to this place of freedom again, her mind recalls how she arrived here – *me first*.

As the echoes of *me first* crowd her thoughts she poses a question. "How can I truly love and give to anyone if I don't know who I am or if I don't know how to love and give to *me first*?" The question drew her back to memories of her grandmother taking the time to teach her about planting a grapevine. She remembered her grandmother explaining how a grapevine has to be nurtured, loved, and cared for first before it can produce good grapes to feed others. The root of the vine must first be anchored into the soil. The soil retains water and nutrients and provides them to the root. In turn, the root releases the required nutrients and water to the vine for the vine's growth. As the vine grows from its supply of sustenance, it is strengthened and eventually will start to cling to surrounding structures like the fence her grandmother used to support the vine. Her grandmother informed her of the various ways to tell when a vine is healthy and true to its nature. She explained how each little bud that sprouted from the vine during the growing process represented another form of life. The vine would first produce leaves and from the leaves would come a flower. Before producing grape berries, the flower *first* has to *self-pollinate* from the nutrients and water provided by the vine, extending from the root, which is anchored in the soil. Each flourishing pollinated flower then becomes a grape berry. The grape berry will ultimately be turned into a cluster of big, sweet, vibrantly colored grapes. Her grandmother shared with her some of the foods grapes are used to make such as jam, raisins, and juice. She smiled at the thoughts. This trip down memory lane gave her a living definition of *me first* and the answer to her life's question.

In order to effectively love anyone, she must learn to adequately love and give to *me first*. Loving *me first* doesn't mean loving *only me*. Actually it means just the opposite. Loving *me first* deepens her love for everyone else and cultivates her desire to passionately give to others what she has given to herself. Like the root of a grapevine anchored in soil, her life must first be anchored in Love, as Love is where she discovers her true identity. Love's water is the stream to her soul that refreshes her character, and Love's nutrients are the delectable delicacies that enlighten her creativity, while nourishing her unique individuality. Just like the vine, this refreshingly enlightened woman is then able to see her true potential and her profitable surroundings. Her new sight is saturated with wisdom and knowledge, which grants her the ability to connect with those who will pull her upward making her more mobile instead of stunting her growth by beating her down. As she associates herself with likeminded individuals who will support her growth and continued maturity, her strength is reinforced by Love's embrace. With Love's embrace and her reinforced strength to grow, her vitality is provoked and produces other various forms of life. She unites this new ability to generate life with her new found joy for living, then out pours clusters of beautifully enriched sources for all to enjoy. Love has become her foundation for life and she lives full of joy.

With Love's bold authority, she gathers her thoughts and verbally releases her truth for all to hear. "*Me first,*" she says in a whisper. Hoping all who were present heard her claim of victory, she awaited their response. But, there was not even a glare in her direction. So, again she declared "*me first.*" This time she spoke with a bit more courage. Some heads turned in her direction with looks of bewilderment. Then, a woman's voice from across the room asked her if she could repeat what she had just spoken. It was as if the woman had been waiting for her to speak. She stood up straight with her shoulders down, head up, eyes fully engaged with the woman, and with a slight arch in her back, she confidently professed in a gentle, yet determined voice, "I have decided to love *me first*, to give to *me first*, and to discover *me first*. I am not claiming to be an independent woman because I know I will need much assistance in my discovery. However, I am convinced that I am more than what I saw and more than what you see in me. This realization has driven me to desire more. Now, I will fulfill my purpose and share with other women how Love reformed me. At last, I understand that before I can invest Love into anyone else's account, I must initially allow Love to take up residency within *me first*."

Who is she? She is me, she is you. She is every woman born of a woman. And, she wants each of us to know the importance of self-love, self-care, and self-giving. Each of these aspects make us better as we learn to give to *"me first"* and this frees us from resentment, hostility, and regret. Taking the time to be filled with Love creates a Christ-assured woman who loves to give Love to others. For most of us, this journey will come at a time and place where we have already poured out so much and because of that, guilt will come knocking. However, guilt is a moral agent resulting from an act of an offense to a crime, knowing it to be a violation of law. To every woman who will read this, there is no law against loving *"me first."* As a matter of fact, the law of Love is Love as Christ loves you. In other words, Love as you have been loved by Love. Therefore, we must let Love, love us first. So, try it! And, let's discover the true essence of internal Love and the joy that comes with it. Then, once we have been filled with Love, let's allow Love to overflow from our hearts to the hearts of everyone else.

Let the Truth Sting

The Next Sip...

There is more to come so please enjoy this sip of the next edition of Coffee Break.

Let the Truth Sting

Black Coffee No Sugar No Cream

"Love suffers long and is kind...does not behave rudely...is not provoked...thinks no evil...bears...hopes...endures...all things. Love never fails..."
1 Corinthians 13:4-8

In the words of my pastor, brother and friend, Dwayne Merritt, "God's not mad at us, He loves us." In order to truly understand the Father, we must first understand Love. In a general sense, Love gives gentle and kind advice without forcing His will on others. Love considers others more than self, doesn't go off when others mess up, nor keeps a record of the mess ups. As a matter of fact, as others are making a mess, Love responds pleasantly, patiently looking for the best, while withstanding the mess. Love doesn't walk away prematurely. He tolerates ALL things, only trusts and believes the truth. Love keeps going all the way to the end because Love NEVER dies. Whenever the Father looks upon those of us who are adopted through Christ, He sees the Love...

...Now, let us ask ourselves, who has been *positioned* in our life for the purpose of us loving "*the mess*" out of them?

Coffee Break

Let the Truth Sting

ABOUT THE AUTHOR

Letitia Doss (*The Coffee Lady*) has been happily married to the love of her life, Shannon Doss, for seventeen years. They have two beautiful daughters, Chantené (18) and Tiana (15), who has been an inspiration for Letitia's writing from the start. Her desire to be an example of a woman, who can live a fulfilled life in Christ, prompted her writing and her willingness to surrender her whole life to God. In moments of what she thought was the greatest pain, God called her to write and out poured several books with two being self published. Letitia is a sought after inspirational speaker and published author. Through speaking and writing she has turned many life obstacles into conquered victories.

For the past nine years her work has impacted various communities of women. In 2006, Letitia Doss published a poetry book that dealt with her pain of being sexually abused. After the completion of her first published book, "Finally Unmasked: Let the Truth Heal" she began speaking at support groups for sexually abused teens. During the time she was a support staff at a non-profit agency. She witnessed numerous cases where sexual abuse was prevalent. This inspired her to research the affects of sexual abuse on women and to find the "life after" statistics of survivors within her present community. The numbers were disheartening, but the research prepared and gave her what she needed to take action. Letitia contacted several non-profit agencies and presented a proposal to assist with their support groups. Some of them allowed Letitia to use her book in different forums and a number of her books were purchased as therapy tools by some of the agencies. Her readings and speaking provided a hopeful outcome for many of the teens who had been victimized. Some of them stated that for the first time they saw themselves getting past what had happened to them. Letitia has maintained relationships with some of the teens and they are now utilizing unique ways to give to others what they believe her work has given to them.

It was during that time when Letitia realized women of all ages could gain insight into their futures and overcome similar pain at any age. Therefore, she started hosting small group meetings for women who were interested in finding new ways to come together and support one another. From those meetings several women went on to open non-profit organizations and for profit businesses using their pain and passion to give back to their communities.

In 2013, a co-worker asked Letitia to speak for a working women's class she taught at Eastern Michigan University. The students in the class were so moved, Letitia was asked to speak regularly each semester. This rekindled her writing. Letitia had been inspired by the responses from the woman, which lead to the completion of several unpublished books.

Finally, in September 2014, Letitia began writing "Coffee Break: Let the Truth Sting" during a time when she was ready to through in the towel and call it quits. After years of giving and going, Letitia discovered she had neglected to give to the one person who needed her the most, herself. During her discovery, she realized this was common amongst most women. The completion of her second book stirred up a desire to empower women, which lead to the development of a program focused on unifying women by exemplifying their uniqueness as individuals and providing platforms for them to share their story. This most recent work also lead to her full acceptance of self and is intended to empower other women in the same way. She has mentored and encouraged women in all walks of life and is steadily looking for opportunities to restore value in worth in all women.

Let the Truth Sting

2nd Edition
Coffee Break: The Misrepresentation of Love
COMING 2016

www.ingramcontent.com/pod-product-compliance
Lightning Source LLC
LaVergne TN
LVHW041233080426
835508LV00011B/1190